1

4

9

3

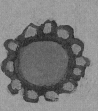

5

2

8

5

7

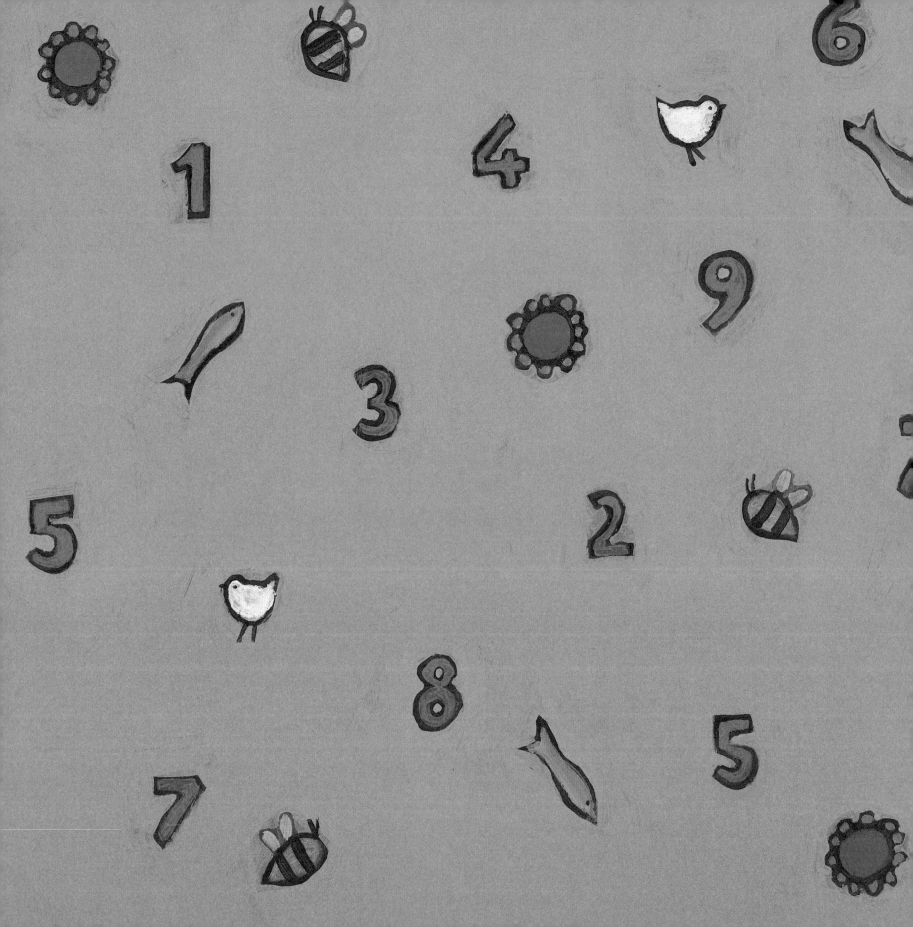

CLEO'S COUNTING BOOK

Caroline Mockford

Barefoot Books
Celebrating Art and Story

Let's count with Cleo from one to ten.

Then let's count back to one again.

6 7 8 9 10

One big gate.

2

Two
small
dogs.

Three
singing
birds.

3

Four
speckled
frogs.

5

Five
stepping
stones.

6

Six tall trees.

7 Seven flashing fishes.

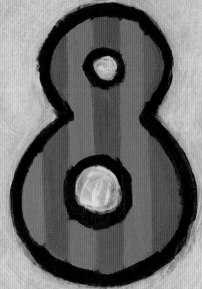

8

Eight
buzzing
bees.

Nine fluffy
chicks —
but where is
mother hen?

Here she comes
with one more
chick — and
that makes ten!

Cleo can count
from one to ten.

1 2 3 4 5

one
two
three
four
five

6 7 8 9 10

six seven eight nine ten

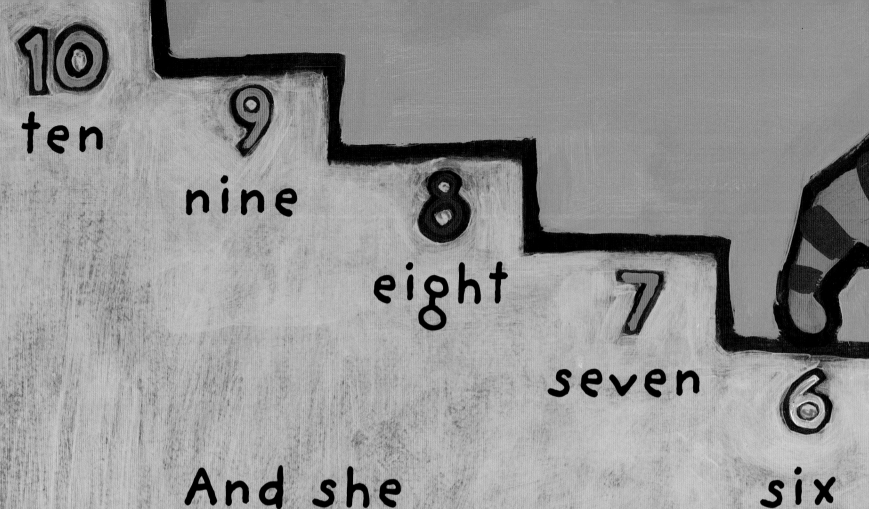

10 ten

9 nine

8 eight

7 seven

6 six

And she can count back to one again!

five

4 four

3 three

5

2 two

one 1

For Freddy and Felix — S. B.
For Phoebe and Hepzibah — C. M.

Barefoot Books
124 Walcot Street
Bath BA1 5BG

This book is printed on 100% acid-free paper
The illustrations were prepared in acrylics on 140lb watercolour paper
Design by Jennie Hoare, Bradford on Avon
Typeset in 44pt Providence Sans Bold
Colour separation by Bright Arts Graphics, Singapore
Printed and bound in Singapore by Tien Wah Press (Pte.) Ltd.

Hardback ISBN 1 84148 206 4

British Cataloguing-in-Publication Data:
a catalogue record for this book
is available from the British Library

1 3 5 7 9 8 6 4 2

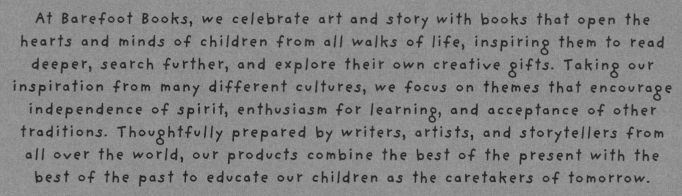

Barefoot Books
Celebrating Art and Story

At Barefoot Books, we celebrate art and story with books that open the hearts and minds of children from all walks of life, inspiring them to read deeper, search further, and explore their own creative gifts. Taking our inspiration from many different cultures, we focus on themes that encourage independence of spirit, enthusiasm for learning, and acceptance of other traditions. Thoughtfully prepared by writers, artists, and storytellers from all over the world, our products combine the best of the present with the best of the past to educate our children as the caretakers of tomorrow.

www.barefootbooks.com

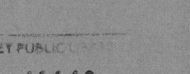

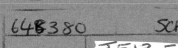

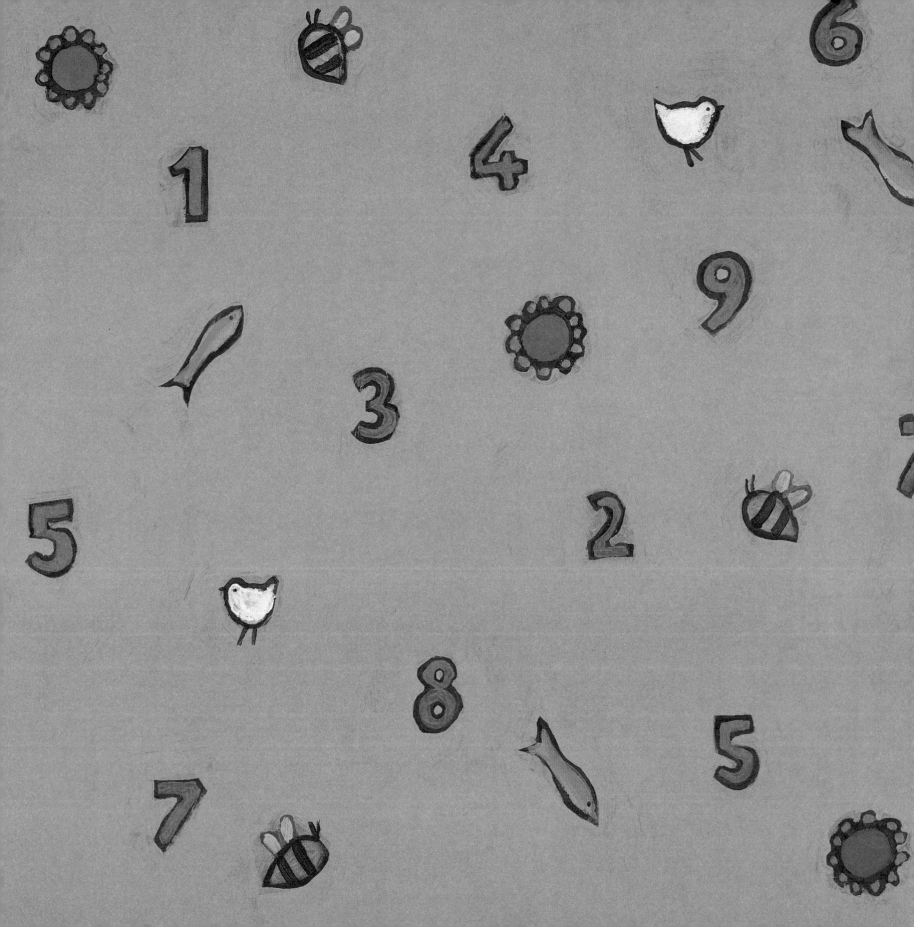